On The Wings ot a Dove

On The Wings of a Dove

June Hopkins

The Pentland Press Limited
Edinburgh • Cambridge • Durham

© June Hopkins 1994

First published in 1994 by
The Pentland Press Ltd.
1 Hutton Close
South Church
Bishop Auckland
Durham

ISBN 1 85821 224 3

Acknowledgement is made to Janet Mason
for her kind help and encouragement.

Typeset by CBS, Felixstowe, Suffolk
Printed and bound by Antony Rowe Ltd., Chippenham

To
My Dad
My Mum
My Family

TO JANET MASON
(who sadly died before this book could be published)

Why oh why does it have to be
When someone as nice as she
Is taken by God with him to abide
And to walk forever by his side
From Janet we could all learn a lot
Like when to complain and when not
She was ill for more than twenty years
And no doubt shed her private tears
Finally God came and took her hand
For he knew her suffering was too much to stand
So she has gone into his eternal care
For her faith alone has got her there
Now she is walking tall and straight
To join her father through the Golden Gates

WALK ON

The first step is a hard step, the hardest step to make,
But each one thereafter is easier to take.
As we walk through life, we don't really see
It is only when troubled that they come back to thee.
Remember only the good, do not cry for the bad,
But be glad you can remember the times you have had –
When you first met and then became a bride,
The many years you have shared side by side.
Now his health is getting a little weak,
And the help of others is what you now seek.
Do not ever forget God is by your side
And from Him there is nothing you can hide.

SUFFERING

You were always a good Christian soul,
When mind and body were truly whole.
But when that was taken away
It was pain and suffering every day.
So God, if you are merciful, always keep
Her in your arms in eternal sleep.

CHRISTMAS PAST

As I remember long past years,
With fun, laughter and a love that cheers.
Christmas was so different when I was small;
No TV or video but fun and games for one and all.
Presents, often home-made, that weren't too dear.
Family and friends would come from far and near.
The food was the same as we have today,
But the games that we would play,
Pass the Parcel, a Beetle Drive –
To get the prize at the end we all would strive.
Mimes and other party games we would play
Alas, not many are played at parties today.
It is computer games and what is on TV.
I wonder what future Christmases will be.
Sometimes I long for the good old days;
At least God is still with us in so many ways.

JOYRIDE

I dare, I dare, I double dare
To take that car that stands over there.
The doors are unlocked, the keys are in,
Now the fun can begin.
We climb inside and start her up
So glad he remembered to fill her up.
Through the lanes and roads we chase,
The cops are behind – let's give them a race.
Seventy, eighty, ninety, a ton,
I wish this race had never begun!
Brake hard – You'll never make that curve!
That other car has had to swerve.
Over the car rolls and round the lamp it's bent.
Police, ambulance and crash crew are in sight
They come upon this terrible plight.
Car so mangled and bodies all smashed,
Bones are broken and head's all gashed.
They have cut the car – now they are all free.
All but one go to the mortuary.
That one is filled with such remorse
That their joyride took such a course.
Nightmares, sadness and a lot of fear too
That I did that dare for you.
You bullied me and now you are dead –
I am crippled and have to be fed.
Drugs, drink and crime – this is the result,
Don't joyride and you will be an adult.

A DREAM

A dream is a dream - it is not real,
So I am the only one to feel
Sadness because it can never come true,
As I didn't share the dream with you.
Is it stupid to want such things
As only hard work and commitment brings?
Is it silly to be a boss of your own
And have a life that others have known?
Am I wrong to want such things
That only money and position brings?
But for me these things will never be
As others do not share the dream with me.

SIDES OF LIFE

What does life hold in store?
Why do some get more and more
While others always want and need
And often have to beg and plead?
Just to get by each day
And nowhere for a head to lay.
It doesn't seem really fair
That the store of life doesn't share.
Why some live in luxury, it is said,
And others have nowhere to lay their head.
Why some live on caviar and cream
For others, a home is but a dream.
Some have good fortune so easily
While others toil unmercifully.
Pain and misery and unhappiness too,
Is what the store of life gives to you.
I suppose life seems unjust –
But we will be equal when we are dust.

MY PLAN

A cheeky grin, a loving smile,
You make life worthwhile.
After all is said and done
You are my grandson.
As you get older and go on life's way,
I hope you will stop and think someday,
Of your old and loving Nan
Into whose arms you often ran.
You'll never know how much you mean to me.
But I hope that I shall see
You grow up to be a man,
And to see your children – that's my plan.

HOME

Is yours a house or is it a home?
Does it shine with happiness as each room you roam?
Bits on the carpet and a cobweb or two,
Windows look dirty as the sun shines through.
Or is it a house, made of brick and wood
That doesn't ring with laughter – as it should?
Only gleam with a shine so deep
That a daily polishing does keep.
If yours is a house, a home or whatever,
I hope love will live there forever.

TO DAD

He was seventeen when he met you
And it proved to be a love so true.
But now that he is dead and gone
His loving memory lingers on.

He worked so hard when we were small
To fulfil the wishes of us all.
As the years slipped slowly by
He helped you toil beneath the sky.

Many found him a friend - honest and true,
With a lot to be learned from a good man too.
But now is the time goodbye to say,
As he comes to the end of his day.

He never did grumble or complain,
As his body was so racked with pain.
It's hard without him for you to go on;
But you must, for June, Mary and John.

And don't forget the grandchildren too,
As we all need the help we can get from you.
Think of all the times that you had.
We all miss our dear, loving, wonderful Dad.

ALWAYS THERE

He will always be with us wherever we look.
What others thought of him would write a book.
He accepted what life had to offer him.
Now he will make a new life for us all,
When one day, our turn will be called.
Goodbye and God bless.

SORRY

Although we can't be with you,
You are only a thought away.
You know you are so precious to us all
Each passing day.
Try not to be too sad,
But look around and you will see,
You are the cover of an open book,
Your family the pages must be.
What you taught us the words are a must
And the pictures are in our minds.
The past year wasn't right or just.
In the future all who come to read your book
And be the kind of people
Like my Dad and Mum.
Happy Christmas.

REMEMBER

I remember when I was a kid
All the things that I did.
Climbing the rafters in the barn,
Being told 'Careful – or you'll come to harm.'
Horses and cows with nice fresh milk,
And baby piglets with skin like silk.
Lots of butter and nice fresh cream.
Alas, now it is just a dream.
We had no TV or hi-fi,
And we didn't wonder why
We had so many repeats,
But still sat goggle-eyed and glued to our seats.
No electric or mod. cons.,
Just a well with an old pump on.
The old wash copper in the corner,
And hot bricks to make the bed warmer.
Home-cured ham and suet pud.
It's the life modern youngsters should
Be able to sample, and I should say
There would be more peace in the world today.

TRUE LOVE

True love needs only a glance
To make you wonder if you stand a chance,
Of spending the rest of your life
Living together as husband and wife.
A love like that is oh, so rare,
Only you two can share.
Even when you're far away
A love like that can never sway,
And when you get to the late, late years,
You have shared the laughter and the tears;
You watched your family come and gone
Knowing that your love lingers on.
Then when the time comes to part,
Know that they will be ever in your heart
To give you strength to carry you through,
Till the time when God calls to you.

A NAN

A cheeky grin and smiling eyes
Are worth more to me than any prize.
When they ask those funny things
About how life begins,
And they have such loving ways,
Oh, the dividend it pays.
When they say 'Give me a cuddle',
Even though you are in a muddle.
It is worth more than a crock of gold
And more than wealth untold,
When they say 'I love you, Nan',
I know how lucky I am.

GARDEN OF EDEN

Shrubs, flowers and many a tree,
There is beauty all around to see.
With all the colours of the rainbow too,
Scattered around for me and you.
Many of us are too blind to see them,
But they are more valuable than any gem.
So wake up before it's too late
And help, a Garden of Eden to create.

FUN

Why can't I be like Peter Pan
And stay just the way I am?
Why does it have to be
That grown-ups don't have fun like me?
My brother and my sister too
Have lots of homework to do.
That's not for me –
Like a bird – I want to be free,
To do just as I like.
Whoops! I fell into a dyke!
It wasn't very deep you see.
It only came to my knee.
Frogs, fishes and insects too,
I know what I will do.
I'll go and show them to my Mum
Then she will know I'm having fun!

GARDENING

As I worked in your garden in the open air
I had the strangest feeling that Dad was standing there.
Watched as I dug the trench and put the compost in,
Then turned the soil upon it and made a trench again.
I wasn't sure I was doing it right, as the sweat dripped off my brow,
So I looked up to the sky to say 'Well, what do you think,
Am I doing this OK?' when suddenly, quick as a blink,
I saw his face and heard him say, 'that's all right – it'll do.'
With a tilt of his head and a sort of smile,
Somehow I just know he is watching over me and you.

GOD?

I wonder if God is really there,
For He certainly didn't hear or care
When I asked Him to spare Dad
The unbearable pain he had.
Now I have asked God to help you
To give you courage to see
You through the night as you must do.
But there - no one listens to me.
You think I am being unkind
And that I really don't mind
The gap there now must be
Without someone as wonderful as he.
But oh yes, I do
For I miss him too.
It's hard for me to say what I feel
And you think I am as hard as steel,
Because I said you must face the night,
But, deep down, you know I am right.

I WILL DO IT

You can't do it. You're not clever, it was said.
So I would go off early to bed.
I did not realize just how they were wrong,
So through life I just drifted along.
Not trying to do better at school;
I was a 'dunce' - that was the rule.
I just drifted along life's way
Until it came, that fateful day
When my Dad took ill and died.
Because of his suffering I could not cry,
Instead my tears came out in rhyme.
Who knows, success may one day be mine.
Stupid and inferior I always felt,
In clever people's company, I would melt.
No more do I feel this way;
I know I WILL make it one day.

APPRECIATION

Why don't we ever admit
That we are not really fit?
Why don't we appreciate
Until it is nearly too late?
To see the beauty all around
And to hear every little sound;
Doing things in everyday life
With no effort or strife.
I now find it hard to walk,
And to hear other people talk.
My eyes are getting quite weak
Stronger glasses are what I seek.
Doing housework makes me puff,
Only a few minutes work and I've had enough.
The weeds in the garden are quite tall –
I dare not do it in case I fall.
As I sit here and reflect,
The only thing I regret
I didn't make the most of things,
Of seeing the beauty that nature brings
Of hearing her every sound,
Of God's creatures on the ground.
If I could live life anew
I know just what I would do,
I'd make the most of every minute
And appreciate all that is in it.

A NEW LIFE

On the 31st of January, 1988,
God opened up a brand new gate.
For Thomas Michael arrived at 6.32.
Now life will have a new meaning for both of you.
Love and guidance in the coming years,
and no doubt you will shed a few tears.
But teach him to know right from wrong,
Then to you he will always belong.
May love always be with you as much as today.
God bless and keep you safe, I pray.

STEPS

Each step you have taken on your own
Is one he would want you to make.
Like when a baby first walks alone,
Uncertain are those steps he takes.
But with love and reassurance from his family
He learns to walk quite happily.
And when you think none is there,
Your love will be sure to hear your prayer,
And help and watch you through the night,
And then in the morning light
You have all his things around,
And remember all the happiness you found
Together, as you walked hand in hand.
Know that he is now in Wonderland
Making a new home for us all,
When God decides us to call.

A DAUGHTER

It was in the year 1959
That I had a daughter, so divine.

With dark curly hair, and big brown eyes.
Oh! The memory of her very first cries.

As she grew up – so kind to others,
And caring, too, of her two brothers.

Now she has a home of her own,
She will know the love I have known.

FREEDOM

If God is merciful as they say
Then why did she suffer in every way?
Not able to do anything for herself
Because of her very poor health.
Give her freedom, if you really do care,
Freedom in heaven with you to share,
Grant her everlasting sleep
And in your arms please always keep.

STRENGTH

I did what I did because I cared,
And it was a love that we both shared.
She taught me all the things I can do,
And gave me the strength to carry me through.
The days when you are no longer there,
But I know that you now will share
The rest of all eternity with your love
In God's house in heaven above.

GOODBYE

Loving husband, father, brother and friend,
He was all of these to the very end.
But do not feel too sad,
Remember the good times in life he had.
Know that he will always watch over you
Giving you the strength to carry you through.
Until the day when you meet again,
And in God's house forever will remain.

WHAT WE SEE

We take for granted when we arise,
The brown of the earth, the blue of the skies.
All the different shades of green,
The thousands of flowers to be seen.
The look of peace on a sleeping child's face –
All of these are God's given grace.
But what of those who cannot see?
What help to them will there be?
A white stick and a guide too,
Is this all the help we can give to you?
If only folk would understand
And sometimes lend a hand.
You know that you are not alone,
From the care that others have shown.

NIGHT FEARS

When at night I couldn't sleep,
Into your bed I would creep.
You would banish all my fears,
With a love that has lasted through the years.
Now, if only I could do the same,
I would banish all your pain.
Give you the peace which you ask –
But that alone is God's task.

MIND AND SOUL

Pain in mind, body and soul,
Remembering when you were completely whole.
Working all the hours of a day,
Many of them without pay.
Lovingly care for your family,
So a better life for them would be.
Now, in final years, you just sit in your chair –
Does anyone really care?

REGRETS

Harsh words are often said
When really they should remain in your head.
Words that hurt and tear you apart.
You often wish you could restart
To the time when you first met.
But now perhaps you regret
Some of the things you did say.
But if there is love at the end of the day,
Then as you get older you get wiser too.
There is companionship between the both of you.
You will look back on these troubled years
And with your family, laugh and say 'Cheers'.

RELEASE

When you are old, ill and very weak
It is release from this world that you seek.
Not drugs and medicines to keep you alive,
For without them they would not thrive.
They often say they want to die,
And beside their loved ones in eternity to lie.
Please give them peace and let them go,
God, please your mercy show.

SLEEP

Sleep now without pain,
United with your love again.
In God's house he waited there
Now for all eternity you both can share.

THE MARATHON

I have just watched the Marathon run,
Some for competition, some for fun.
Men, women and wheelchairs too
All have over 26 miles to do.
There are hundreds and hundreds at the start,
Very eager to take part.
A lot of money is raised each year
And all for charity, that is very clear.
For this alone it helps them on,
On this London Marathon.
When the end is in sight
They all know they were right
To put up with all the pain,
And – yes – they will do it again.

TIME

On this final day, don't be too sad.
For it was a good long life he had.
Remember your time together with pride,
When you walked hand in hand by his side.
Think of those days and be glad
For the time together you have had,
Know that he is now by God's side,
To await for his loved ones in God's home to abide.

SUNSHINE

Why do we feel miserable and glum
When there is no sun?
Why do we feel happy and gay
When the sun shines all day?
It really is heaven sent,
And on earth we are only lent.
So accept each day for what it is;
We only get out what each of us gives.

SELF

I know I am not much to look at,
And I am not very intelligent.
I have always had a brain that's not all there,
But I have got a heart that really does care.
I don't have a way with fancy words,
Or a very high IQ.
I found school a terrible chore, and how
Things might have been different now.
But it is too late for me to do
Anything about it so,
I must put up with it
And make a go.

DEATH

After we are dead and gone,
I hope fond memories linger on.
Don't rant or make a fuss
Over things that belonged to us.
Please take an equal share
Of all that is in there.
Know that I have loved you all and cared,
That the future will always be shared.
You will be the best of friends
We learn too late - when a life ends.
God bless and goodbye.
Please do not cry.

CAN YOU HEAR ME?

Can you hear me when I sing?
Free me from sorrow, free me from sin.
Can you hear me when I pray
Of all the things I meant to say?
Can you hear me when I ask
Your help in doing that difficult task?
Can you hear what I just said
Even though your body is dead?

Your soul and memory will ever be
Within the very heart of me.
I know you can hear it all
And you answer us when we call.
We may not always agree –
But God knows best for you and me.

THE WEDDING

It was on the 29th January 1985
The lives of you two came alive.
For it was then that you two were wed.
Now you have the rest of your lives ahead
The love that you shared on that day,
May it always, forever, remain that way.
Often you will be miles apart,
But be ever in each other's heart.

IN THE NAVY

I have a son whose name is Paul,
He is fair and he is tall.
Such a good and thoughtful lad
Just the same as my dear Dad.
The Navy was the job he chose,
And I'm sure he knows
That one day I hope I will see
Him with his own family.
I hope she will love him,
Then his cup of happiness will be full to the brim.

GRANDAD

My Dad was great and didn't say much,
But was always truthful, honest and such.
A good and kind, gentle man was he.
Alas, he is now just a memory,
Of day at work in fields so dusty,
Of caring for his machinery so it never went rusty,
Of things he did for us when we were small;
Our wishes he tried to grant them all.
There's so much more I could tell,
Stand on a hilltop and yell.
I don't think I really did see
That others thought the same as me.
I am so grateful he was my Dad.
I will try to live the same as he had.

PAUL

Oh, how wonderful when you were young,
That you were mine on a September day.
The joy when I felt you move inside
And when you were born your lungs opened wide.
As a baby you needed me so,
And with a loving heart I watched you grow.
I helped you through the good and bad.
I am thankful for the days I have had.
On that day you went to sea
I knew you were gone from me.
You have now started your very own book –
Occasionally, stay and look
At those you have left behind,
You will always be on my mind.

PAUL AND PENNY

It's hard to say just how I feel
At the moment it seems unreal.
When you went away, you were my son,
Now you belong to another one.
I had hoped that I would see
You take your vows, just like me.
Dressed in your number one suit,
With Penny in white and looking cute,
A church, a party, family and all,
With photographs, so you could recall
The day you took your wedding vow.
But it is so much different now.
I wish you both lots of happiness,
And that God will truly bless
All your married life –
Paul and Penny, who is now your wife.

CHRISTIANS

You hear people say they are Christians,
But what does it really mean?
Is it that they have something to believe in?
Are they better than they have been?
Some never go into a church,
While others go nearly every day,
But they haven't left God or the Church
While some of the others may.
What a terrible world, some folk say,
With violence and death every day.
Some live with that constant threat,
While others – it's food they can't get.
But it's the good deeds that folk do
And never ask for repayment.
For God, they still look up to you,
And what they say is really meant.

TEARS

One little hankie to wipe away the tears,
As you remember all the past years.
Tears will not mend a broken heart
Nor take away the pain,
But faith in God is just the start
Of learning how to live again.
If there is another life,
And I firmly believe that's so,
Then he has gone to build a life
Until it is time for us all to go.

PEACE

She was so good and so kind
She will be badly missed by those left behind.
She did everything that she could,
The wrongs of others on her shoulders stood.
But now, at last, she is at peace.
No pain or worry, just perfect peace.

FOOTPRINTS

I used to walk in freshly washed sand
And dream I was exploring a strange new land.
People would come from miles around
Just to see the treasures I had found.
Also, with face aglow
I would make footprints in the snow,
Pretend I was in the Arctic waste –
Nearly time for tea – I have to make haste.
Now I am old I still do these things
But it is only memories the footprints bring.

LOVE

I know you have a wife and family too,
And that they mean so much to you.
But I hope one day to share
For I have a lot of love to spare.
I hope I can love them before it's too late,
And God hasn't closed my final gate.
And I'm in the garden where flowers never die,
Only sweetly singing birds, and no need to cry.
I am very glad you are my son,
This is from your loving Mum.

TIME

Time has a habit of marching on.
When time is over it's really gone.
We can never get it back again,
Only remember – and often with pain.
You think of time when it's getting late,
But time marches on – it doesn't wait.
Make the most of the time left to you.
Work hard, be honest and sensible too.
Keep your promise and be very kind
To other folk, and you may find
That you have time to spare,
Time to love, time to share.

IRELAND

What is the reason, does no one really care
About the many killings; or just glad we are not there?
Have they forgotten why it all started?
Have brains and common sense departed?
Martyrs are not those who have been killed,
But all whose blood by others has been spilled.
For what cowards they really are,
To hide their faces and stand from afar.
A bomb hurts the innocent and causes such pain,
The killer says sorry, then does it again.
I think that God has forsaken thee.
Until you can all live in harmony.
Talk to each other over the garden gate,
Not teach your children from birth to hate.
To be able to go anywhere without fear,
To be able to talk and make your views clear.
To know that you can sleep in your own bed
And not step on a bomb or get a bullet in the head.
I think that they are just a few
Who have put the fear of God into you.
If enough of you who are innocent and good,
Turn on the bad – like you should,
Then your country will be as you planned –
A United Ireland.

CHRISTMAS

In the year of 1984
We all came through your door
We came for one reason –
To celebrate the Christmas season.

The food, the presents, the spirit of cheer,
That brings families so near.
Even though some are miles away,
We think of them more on this day.

Carols, tinsel and fairy lights
Glistening in the dark of night,
Just like the star which shone so long ago,
To tell of the birth of Jesus, you know.

It is why we remember each year
The ones who cannot be here.
We hope that next year brings
Peace and Happiness and all good things.

TROUBLES

Life does not seem to be fair
With all the trouble you have to bear.
To some, success comes at the drop of a hat,
Only bills and worry drop on your mat.
But turn to God and say a prayer,
For I am sure he knows you are there.
He gives you the strength to carry on.
Laugh, and your troubles will be long gone.

TRYING

It feels to you that God does not care,
For worry and trouble you have more than your share.
Just as things are going right
And success is coming and you just might
Be able to climb the ladder of life
And to live in comfort without any strife;
Then something happens to pull you back
And you wonder just what it is you lack.
But not for long are you that way
And down the bottom you will not stay.
Take a look at your loved ones and smile,
To the top you will get in a little while.
I know that God is watching you
Helping in all you do.

MONEY

Money is the root of all evil, so it is said,
And the road to ruin many have been led.
While at school when money was tight,
Your parents taught you wrong from right.
Then you get a job with plenty of cash,
And so behave a little rash.
Drinking, smoking, dining out and a new car –
You soon find your money doesn't go very far.
You borrow money to pay the bill,
The worry of it makes you ill.
Things seem to go from bad to worse
And you begin to realize money is a curse.
So stop and think – and make your plans,
Your destiny is in your own hands.
Work and save and your dreams will come true,
So now it is all up to you.

DON'T BE SAD

Don't be sad now she is no longer near;
Do not cry or shed a tear.
Just remember she is now in God's care
And His love forever will share.
Of memories there will be plenty,
So don't let your heart feel empty.
I am sure she is watching over all her family
And will do so for all eternity.

ALL ALONE

How lonely life must be
With no one to talk to thee.
Just a voice on the phone
Who doesn't care that you are alone.
Just excuses why they didn't come.
It doesn't matter that you are their Dad or Mum.
One day they will be just like you,
Perhaps will be very lonely too.
Then will they remember your lonely days
And the help they could have given in many ways;
Will their family, too, not care,
Just phone to see if they are still there?
Don't leave it until it's too late –
Go now – and make it a regular date.

IN MEMORY OF A CHELSEA PENSIONER

When I saw you there racked with pain,
And knew that you would never again
Wear your coat of brilliant red,
Or put the Tricorn hat upon your head.
But now at last you are free
To live with God for all eternity.
To join your wife who has gone before
And waits for you near heaven's door.
Where, you can take her hand
And walk together in God's promised land.

Can you hear me when I sing
In church, your favourite hymn?
Can you hear just what I say
As I kneel down to pray?
I feel that you are standing by that stone,
Near to God's heavenly throne.
Watching over us every day, so
When it's time for us to go
We will have nothing to fear,
Because we know you are always near.

ROOTS

You started off as just a seed,
Was loved and cared for so you would succeed
In planting roots of your own,
And like a giant oak tree, you have grown.
The main branches - your children must be;
And the little boughs - their family.
Many things in the past you have done
Since the year 1891.
Many changes in your home;
Gone the oil lamps and candles you have known,
Washers, Hoovers and TV too
To make life easier for you.
With such a big family, you are a success.
Only left to say is Good Luck and God Bless.

THE GARDEN

If I was to win - how happy I would be
A 'handicapped' garden I would pick you see.
Don't do the garden, my husband was told,
If you want to walk when you get old.
He's tried at times, but in vain
As this only causes a lot of pain.
Over twenty years I have soldiered through,
Till age and health both catch up with you.
Why is it that weeds seem to grow,
Before the flowers have time to show?
My garden is quite large you see
And gets bigger each year, it seems to me.
So, a garden that's easy for my old age –
My gratitude would fill a book's every page!

OUR QUEEN

You have been our Queen for many years,
And shown only happiness - never tears.
Your life has been like an open book,
The whole world taking a look.
No walking like lovers down a leafy lane;
Never showing that you have some pain.
But, while you are fit in body and mind,
Stay as our Queen - if you would be so kind.
And when the time comes for you to retire,
Put on your slippers and sit by the fire,
And let others do all you used to do
Until God's call comes to you.

SUFFERING

Very little I have cried
Since the day that he died;
But my tears will be unshed
As I lay awake in bed.
God doesn't hear or care
Because I don't think he is there.
So I will suffer alone,
And one day, maybe, I can atone
For the hurt I have caused you.
But you know, what Dad would want you to do,
I will keep my promise to Dad
And keep his garden the way he had.
For when I am down there
I am close to him,
So it is easier to bear.
I am what I am because of you and him.

CONSECRATION OF A TOMBSTONE

Do not be sad on this Blessing Day.
Smile, as together the prayers you say.
For your love has gone to make a new home,
And you know you are never alone.
For she will always look down upon you,
Guiding you in all you do.
Waiting until she is by your side once again,
When hand in hand you both forever will remain.

TRY TO UNDERSTAND

It is very hard to understand why
Your loving husband and father had to die.
You only know the empty pain
Of learning how to live again.
Know that he is ever close to,
As he ever watches over you,
Helping you through the coming days –
Always with you in so many ways.
Have faith in God, and you will see
Him again, in heaven for all eternity.
God bless you all.

GETTING OLD

Who will look after me now I'm old and infirm?
Who will show me some concern?
Get my pension and some shopping too,
And don't forget, there's my housework to do.
Oh! I forgot. You don't do it anymore.
Just leave the dirt upon the floor.
I used to keep it ever so clean
Your face in the furniture could be seen.
Now come and look and you will see
Just what has become of me,
Back is bent, my body weak,
It was only some help I seek.
I've been to the doctor, he gave me some pills.
They are supposed to cure all ills.
Water in puffy legs and feet,
Spend more time upon your seat.
There's arthritis in back, arms and knees,
But it's walk and exercise if you please.
I talk to myself, as no one will come.
Being alone is not much fun.
Perhaps it is right, what has been said,
People like me are better off dead.